P E T E R   L I K

"My total dedication and obsession with photography has taken me on journeys into many remarkable areas throughout Australia.
I captured this collection of images using a specialist panoramic camera. Because of the wider field of view, this format enables me to portray the true spirit of Australia on film. Upon viewing these images I am sure you will share with me the tranquillity and solitude I experienced whilst exploring the stunning beauty of this country."

peter lik PUBLISHING

PO Box 2529 Cairns Queensland 4870 Australia
Telephone: (07) 4053 9000 **Fax:** (07) 4032 1277
sales@peterlik.com.au   **www.peterlik.com**

© **Peter Lik Publishing**   BK08
ISBN 0 958 7002 22

Front cover - Twilight over Sydney Harbour
Back cover - Aerial view of Sydney

Sydney

PETER LIK

Sydney

THE HARBOUR CITY

Sydney, Australia's largest city and home of the 2000 Olympics, was the first site of the European settlement on the Australian continent. The magnificent coves and waterways of Port Jackson were first discovered in 1770 by Captain James Cook and later declared by Captain Arthur Philip in1788 as the "finest harbour in the world".

The diverse foreshore traverses over 250km of sandy beaches, idyllic harbours, protected coves and around to the thundering surf and awesome cliffs of Watsons Bay.

Today approximately four million people enjoy the lifestyle of this magnificent city. The bustling Sydney Harbour is constantly travelled by ferries, yachts, catamarans, cruise ships and cargo vessels. The lifestyle of Sydneysiders revolve around the water and harbour activities, from dining at a waterfront cafe, sailing in one of the famous yacht races, surfing or relaxing on pristine surf beaches.

Dwarfed by the city skyscrapers, the old world charm of sandstone cottages and warehouses can be seen at the Rocks. Here the oldest part of Sydney can now be enjoyed by fine dining and superb shopping.

The world famous Opera House and Sydney Harbour Bridge, perched upon the sheltered waters of Sydney Cove, are architectural masterpieces that make Sydney, the most beautiful harbour city in the world.

World renowned architecture of the Sydney Opera House.

Centrepoint Tower rises above the city.

Bustling Circular Quay is the heart of Sydney's harbour activity.

Historic tall ships dwarf the Sydney skyline.

Manly Beach displays its glory with Sydney in the background.

Sunset hues over a quaint old jetty, Scotland Island.

The Watsons Bay lighthouse proudly guards the precipitous cliffs of South Head.

Aerial view of Bondi Beach.

The famous swimming pool at Bondi.

A panoramic vista of Sydney - Australia's harbour city.

The sparkling Star City Casino by day.

Glistening steel structure of the Anzac bridge.

The Monorail meanders through the city centre.

Sydney captured from Kirribilli.

Glowing city lights enhance the beauty of the Opera House.

A tugboat bursts through early morning fog.

My favourite shot of Sydney - a pastel skyline.

Twilight reflections, Darling Harbour.

Moonlight casts its glow over the calm waters of Sydney Cove.

The diverse architecture of Sydney.

The Rocks viewed from Observatory Hill.

Sydney ferries cross the harbour in unison.

Aqua waters of Manly beach.

Sydney ferry departs Manly harbour.

Aerial view over Camp Cove and Watsons Bay.

Yachts nestled at The Spit.

A classic ferry transfers locals to Scotland Island.

Turquoise waters of Manly Cove provide the idyllic anchorage.

Sunrise cloud patterns decorate the Olympic City.

A cruise ship rests beneath streaky skies.

Sydney's harbour cradles the famous Opera House and Sydney Harbour Bridge.

A historic fort guards the shores of Bare Island.

Convict castle at La Perouse, Botany Bay.

Majestic Hyde Park fountain beneath Centrepoint Tower.

Morning light filters through trees at the Botanical gardens.

Sandstone buildings retain the pioneering spirit of the first fleet convicts.

The Museum of Contemporary Art overlooks Sydney Cove.

Sunset from "Bridgeclimb".

"Bridgeclimbers" appear as ant like figures on the Harbour Bridge.

The ultimate view of Sydney, captured from "Bridgeclimb" - at the pinnacle of the Harbour Bridge.

The charm of Sydney reflected in the tranquil waters of Port Jackson.

Aerial view of Sydney featuring the Opera House.

Yachts cruise past Sydney's skyline.

Harbour parklands at Blues Point.

Dawn beneath the arch of Sydney Harbour Bridge.

peter lik GALLERY

www.peterlik.com

Multi award-winning photographer Peter Lik proudly presents his signature Galleries. The Galleries, with their handcrafted timber floors and unique custom decor radiate a beautiful ambience.

The stunning 'Gallery Collection' is selected from Peter's library of over 250,000 images and printed as limited edition photographs.

Entering a Peter Lik Gallery is a total sensory experience. His connection with the heart and soul of the landscape is evident and he captures the true feeling of the land like no other.

CAIRNS
4 Shields Street
Tel **(07) 4031 8177**

NOOSA
9 Hastings Street
Tel **(07) 5474 8233**

PORT DOUGLAS
19 Macrossan Street
Tel **(07) 4099 6050**

SYDNEY
QVB, 455 George St
Tel **(02) 9269 0182**

HAWAII USA
712 Front St Lahaina Maui
Tel **(808) 661 6623**

BOOKS BY PETER LIK

- Australia
- Blue Mountains
- Brisbane
- Byron Bay
- Cairns
- Daintree and Cape Tribulation
- Fraser Island
- Gold Coast
- Great Barrier Reef
- Port Douglas
- Sunshine Coast
- Sydney
- The Red Centre
- Townsville and Magnetic Island
- Whitsundays
- Wildlife
- World Heritage Rainforest

LARGE FORMAT PUBLICATIONS

- Australia - Images of a Timeless Land
- Spirit of America

peter lik PUBLISHING